HOW TO BEGIN A
WIDOWS
MINISTRY

HOW TO BEGIN A
WIDOWS
MINISTRY

MARLENE CRAFT

Foreword by Doug Clay

MEDIA.COM

HOW TO BEGIN A
WIDOWS
MINISTRY

Published by
Illumify Media Global
www.IllumifyMedia.com
"Let's bring your book to life!"

Library of Congress Control Number: 2022917747

Paperback ISBN: 978-1-955043-81-6

Typeset by Art Innovations (http://artinnovations.in/)
Cover design by Debbie Lewis

Printed in the United States of America

CONTENTS

ACKNOWLEDGMENTS

Many churches, denominations, and widows have poured into the creation of this guide. This is not one person's opinion or experience, but rather, it is a combination of decades of ministry and dozens of people's experiences gathered into a single tool to equip the local body of believers to create a widows' ministry within their community. We want to thank each person who has been part of this process.

A very huge thank-you to a gentleman who offered to do a matching fund donation, which encouraged people to get on board. Through the giving of many generous hearts and churches, we were able to raise the funds so we could get the program published and into the hands of churches.

My family has been a tremendous tower of strength and wisdom throughout the entire process of writing. Both of my sons played strategic roles within this five-year process. My youngest son, Brian, has been part of the Widows Link team since its inception. His design skills along with his heart for widows has been vitally instrumental in this final product. My oldest son, Chris, has shared his wisdom and given counsel in so many areas. My sister, Lori, has been my constant cheerleader, always encouraging me to go forward with what the Lord has called me to do. I am so blessed to have so many who have prayed and encouraged me through this journey.

A huge appreciation for the Widows Link board who has been in our corner cheering us on through the bumps and challenges we have faced through the years. Thank you for your hearts to bless this ministry.

Thank you to the churches, districts, and many partners who have supported us with your prayers, love, and financial support through the years. It is because of each one of you that we now have a tool that churches can use to minister to widows. There are no words that can express the deep appreciation and love that I feel for each of you who have given toward this project. Know that you play a role in the lives of widows who will be changed for eternity. One day our heavenly Father will reward you. With all my heart I say, "Thank you!"

FOREWORD

To understand how to begin any ministry, you must have the *why* clearly defined. As Christians we all look to God's Word to define the *why* for our lives; however, that doesn't mean we always do what we are called to do. Sometimes this is because we are not sure how to get started; other times we don't feel worthy; still other times we have not been given the tools to accomplish the task to which we have been called.

This is the primary reason that Marlene Craft has written this guide. Widows and widowers are persons with great potential; I know, I was raised by a widow. Marlene desires us to harness the wealth of these individuals and equip them to reach their redeemed potential. Clearly, the Bible calls us to take care of these precious people, and taking care of them means helping them to find their calling. In this book you will hear and feel God's call to His people to take care of widows, both for their good and for His glory. You will find that *you* are worthy—not just the pastorate and not just the staff in our churches, but *you* can assist in this kingdom work. You will be equipped with tools and ideas and will be reminded that you are not alone; all of God's people are called to participate in some way in taking care of widows.

Ephesians 2:10 reminds us that God has prepared good deeds for us to do. And those deeds are still in play at every age and stage of life. Marlene desires to empower you to action through this great resource.

As you read this work, I'm confident you will feel called to respond.

— **Doug Clay,** *General Superintendent*
for the Assemblies of God

INTRODUCTION

This guide is created to shorten the points between the *desire* for a widows' ministry and the *implementation* of an effective ministry where widows' lives are being changed forever in local churches.

In the first two chapters we will look at why there is a need for a widows' ministry, helping you to understand what widows experience so you can better understand their journey. You will hear about their struggles and how they have worked through them by connecting with others who have walked the path of widowhood. As you begin to travel through this guide and embark on this incredible endeavor to change the lives of widows within your community, it may get a little overwhelming. Hear this up front: **you can do this**! You can do all things through Christ who will strengthen you.

Within this guide, you will find information on how to best approach ministry to widows. We will go over the pain widows feel so you can have a better understanding of their journey. Also, we'll talk about what the Bible has to say about widows, and then we will give instructions to help you in launching your widows' ministry. Years of preparation and ministry experience have gone into the information collected in this guide. We are compiling it all in one place so you have all you need to hit the ground running.

Beyond just information and a plan, we want to equip each of you with additional resources that will assist in your journey. From blank forms to creative group activities, we have done our best to equip you to have an effective and Christ-centered ministry within your community. All of the blank documents at the back of this guide are available for free download digitally at WidowsLink.org.

This guide was written to equip churches to do their widows' ministry in a small group format. Jesus used small groups to disciple twelve men who changed the world. His model seems to have worked pretty well.

We have seen over the years how important relationships are in creating real change and lasting ministry within the church. No people group needs relationships more than widows. Since each widow has lost someone of great importance, which creates a huge gap, we help to bridge that gap in two ways. First, we help in bridging the gap of that relationship between the widows and their Creator God. We do this by discussing God's promises in the context of small groups. Secondly, we bridge that gap through connecting them with other widows who have experienced the same pain.

Widows Link exists to equip the local body of Christ to reach, care, and empower widows around the world. This begins with you, the local church or Christian organization leader. Throughout this guide, we will speak to the person who will direct the widows' ministry. If you are a pastor, this will be an incredible resource for the lay leader you feel God is appointing to head up this ministry in your local church. You will be able to hand this guide to the leader, which will walk them, step by step, through the process of starting a widows' group.

One of the primary reasons this guide now exists is to help resource you with everything you will need to get a widows' group started, except for prayer, a leader, and the Lord's timing. Having a successful ministry is not about numbers or budgeting; it is about walking out the steps in the path God has set before you.

We are excited to be partnering with you during this time of growth and new adventure. God is going to do great things through your widows' ministry.

We pray this program equips, informs, and ignites the passion for widows' ministry in you.

CHAPTER 1

BECOMING AWARE OF THE UNTOLD STORIES

Joann's Story: "Who will grieve with me?"

Eleven years ago, Joann and her husband were just beginning to enjoy those wonderful "retirement years" that everyone looks so forward to. Their home was paid off. They had a nice nest egg, and they could travel to see their family and visit the many places they dreamed of seeing.

What a picturesque life they were blessed with!

But all of that was shattered one day when, sitting in a doctor's office, they got the report that her precious husband, Buddy, had Alzheimer's. They had no idea what was ahead, but they would face it together.

Some journeys are short, but not this one. It was a long, hard ten years of watching her life partner slowly lose his memory, with many ups and downs and both good days and bad days. As time went on and he got worse, there were painful days when he said ugly things that she knew he would never say if he was in his right mind. Real heartbreak came when he did not even recognize who she was.

As the disease got worse, the time came when she could no longer care for him at home, and she had to make that hard decision to admit him into a nursing home. The cost of the nursing home nibbled away at their savings like termites eating away at their foundation. The day came when their savings were gone, and the nursing home informed her she needed to sign over their home.

Joann cried out to God pleading that she would not lose her home. That was the very symbol of what they had built together. God in His mercy took Buddy home to heaven before she lost her home.

Joann had lost her love of fifty years. But at least she still had her house. However, that very home became a cave of darkness where she hid away from the world. She had no desire to face a reality that did not include the love of her life.

The thought of getting in her car alone and going out would mean she would have to resign herself to the fact that she was indeed by herself, no longer going shopping or out to eat with Buddy.

No, it was easier on her heart just to stay inside her home and remember how wonderful things used to be. She could look at pictures and imagine him sitting in his chair. Outside the safety of her walls she knew she would see couples talking and laughing together. That would be a painful knife to her soul reminding her of what she no longer had. People called to invite her out, but she chose to stay within the safety of her memories.

So often, it seems easier for widows to shrink into their pain and hurt. Many spend years in isolation, never feeling they can be whole again. Pain and loneliness keep many widows from living out their lives with purpose and joy.

Joann spent the next eight months within the protective walls of her home. A friend invited Joann to come to our widows' small group. I remember the first time she walked into our meeting. You could see the grief pouring from her soul. She cried off and on and did not speak much at all. Yet she felt they really cared about her.

Joann decided to come back the following week. Again the tears rolled, and she opened up a little, telling us about Buddy. The ladies lovingly listened and were able to share in their understanding of what she was going through. It was the same pain they felt after their husbands died.

A special friendship is built as widows open their hearts and share with those who understand the agony they feel. Many family members don't understand, for they have not lost their life partner.

As Joann continued to come to our meetings, she began opening up more and more.

I recall the first time I saw a smile come across her face. It was a joyous day! Some of the ladies at the meeting had brought fresh homemade cookies to share. Janet had brought her favorite homemade cinnamon rolls for her new family of ladies.

Chatter and laughter filled the room as the women shared what had happened during the week. Joann told everyone about the joy of bringing lovely pots of spring daisies to shut-ins in her neighborhood. She shared how one lady had not heard from her family for two weeks, so Joann's smiling face was like a ray of sunshine to her.

Joann became one of our most faithful members. I remember the time when we were scheduled to take a train ride, but it was pouring rain. When I arrived, the railroad parking lot was almost empty, yet there was Joann, ready to board the train. She and I had a lovely time together, even in the midst of the pounding rain. After a couple of months, I noticed that Joann was now reaching out to the new widows attending. She was connecting to them and helping them to feel comfortable.

One of the goals of Widows Link is to help widows discover that God still has a purpose for their lives. Joann approached me one week and asked me to pray with her about discovering what God wanted her to do with her life now. About a month later she came to me with a big smile on her face. She shared with me that she believed the Lord wanted her to visit shut-ins and to minister to them. She now had a new purpose for her life!

Janet's Story: "I miss my family."

I've heard people say about widows, "They have family to take care of them." But even if a widow has family nearby, they usually have busy lives of their own. However, there are some widows who have the disadvantage of not having family close by.

Janet ran some apartment complexes, which kept her a little occupied after her husband died, yet trying to fill her day seemed like a chore. She only had one son, and he lived on the other side of the country, so missing seeing him and her granddaughter added to the loneliness of missing her husband. She wanted to feel like she had a connection. Her search led her to a divorce recovery group. She enjoyed going to the meetings and being around the people but soon realized they didn't understand what she was experiencing and vice versa.

I invited her to come with me to our widows' small group. Though she was a little apprehensive, she thought being around others who had experienced what she was walking through might be a good match. The first time she came to our meeting, she seemed to go around and talk with several of the ladies. It surprised me to see how open she was to talking with everyone. I will always remember the huge smile on her face at the end of that meeting. She came up to me and gave me a big hug, saying, "I finally found a family!" It brought tears to my eyes knowing that a group of widows could indeed be a family to those who needed comfort and understanding.

Angela's Story: "What am I to do now being alone with a 3 year old?"

Angela was a workaholic, a wife, and a mother to their three-year-old daughter. She and her husband, Wayne, went out to celebrate his birthday at a great all-you-can-eat restaurant. He struggled to eat anything. They decided to have him checked out, only to get the results of him having a grapefruit-size tumor on his stomach that was inoperable. Hospice was called in, and just one month later he died. Suddenly, Angela was a single mom tied down to a full-time job. What was she to do? Her commitment to her job was one that had filled her life. Yet she realized that she was now going to have to be intentional about "being there" for her daughter and taking care of herself too.

She connected with a widows' group at her church. Though most of them were much older, they were able to comfort her and share with her their wisdom that they had learned in their journey. She recognized she needed to be fully present with her daughter, while also taking time for herself. She saw that she needed to readjust her priorities and to back away from working so much. Angela's mother became a widow six months after Wayne died, so they moved in together. Her mother also joined the widows' group and eventually became the leader of their group.

Peach's Story: "I'm not sure how to connect."

Recently I was invited to speak at a banquet for widows in northern Alabama. Before the event started, the pastor introduced me to an extremely shy lady. Peach had only been a widow for a short time, but it appeared to me as if life had really beaten her up.

After my talk, I invited the women to consider joining us for our yearly widows' cruise.

A friend at the banquet talked to Peach about the two of them going together on the cruise. When Peach said she couldn't afford it, her friend persisted, suggesting that they do some fundraisers.

On the day of the cruise, many of us caravanned for half a day to get to the port. On the way, I observed Peach. She offered to help when others needed assistance. Also, she began talking to some of the other widows. In amazement, I watched her come alive in a way that was not visible a few months before.

This change continued throughout the cruise, culminating with her sharing a poem she wrote to thank everyone for the week. She even agreed to my request to read it at our last get-together on board.

And the story gets even better.

In the following months, Peach and her friend from the cruise began a small group ministry to widows in their neighborhood. To this day she continues to call and check on them. What a beautiful example of the transformation that can occur when widows connect with other widows.

Marlene's Story: "Who am I without him?"

Most couples don't even want to think about their partner dying. Many times I've heard the phrase "We plan on dying together."

Unfortunately that rarely happens. Eighty percent of the time it is the husband who dies first.[1] I had not given a lot of thought to this during our thirty-two years of marriage. Yet one thing I did was give my husband and my two boys constantly to the Lord. God had blessed me with them, but I realized they were still His.

That was very helpful when on January 1, 2011, the Lord began laying it on my heart that He was going to take my husband home to heaven, even though he was healthy. Walking with the Lord for over fifty years, I have come to trust my Abba Father through many rough storms. I reminded myself that my husband, Wayne, was not mine; he belonged to the Lord. So I accepted the Holy Spirit's words and decided that if God was going to take him home soon, I would create some memories I could recall forever. At different times I would stop and take a picture in my mind, creating a memory.

On January 15, 2011, Wayne and I headed to Montgomery, Alabama, for a wonderful date together. We had received some unexpected money in the mail and there were some gifts we wanted to buy. As we were driving, I reached over and grabbed Wayne's thumb. He looked over at me and said, "What is it?" As I looked up at my precious husband, I answered, "Nothing, I just love you so much!" I was creating a memory. Then I prayed quietly, "Lord, whenever you decide to take him home, please let it be quick. Don't let it be over a long period of time."

Eight hours later we arrived home, tired and worn-out from a long day of shopping. We decided to take a nap before dinner. I laid down and quickly fell asleep. When I woke up, I found Wayne at the computer. While I was asleep, he had downloaded all the pictures of our family from Thanksgiving and Christmas. I grabbed a chair, and we enjoyed looking through all the memories from the past two months: our daughter-in-law's graduation, Thanksgiving, Wayne and our two boys all riding motorcycles together, and the pictures of our joyous time with Wayne's family at Christmas.

Then we went out to the backyard, and as we were talking, Wayne began feeling strange. He began taking long, deep breaths hoping that would help. I asked if I should take him to the hospital. He suggested he first sit down for a few minutes. While he rested on the back steps, I went inside to call 911. When I returned to the porch, his body was beginning to stiffen up like a robot. I pulled him down to the ground and began doing CPR. But then I noticed that his face was turning purple. I thought, *You're taking him home, Lord.*

So I brought him up in my arms and began rocking his stiff body, praying, "Lord, I trust you completely. My life is yours. My future is yours. I trust you fully." Then like a soft blanket being laid over my body, God's peace settled on me, peace that I cannot explain. It was like the Bible talks about, "the peace of God, which surpasses all understanding" (Philippians 4:7 NKJV).

God's peace continued to rest on me, but the hard fact was, Wayne was gone. I was by myself. One day I was a pastor's wife; the next day, I had no husband, no church, no home, and half my income was gone.

All the emotions that flood a widow's mind would fill a library. Instantly their life changes. Many women walk through years of an illness with their spouse, knowing that one day he will die. Still, when it finally happens, their world is turned upside down. No one is there to sit across the table from you at breakfast. The bed feels so big and causes your heart to break knowing he will no longer be lying beside you.

You are left to figure out who you are without your husband. I *loved* being a pastor's wife. It is *who* I was. No longer a pastor's wife, who am I? Just me, by myself?

There are new stories to write, and we need you to help us do it.

These are just a few of the testimonies of the great things we have seen as widows come together in small groups. This is our passion behind this book.

Our desire is to light a fire within your heart to minister to these precious ladies. Do you want to make a difference?

After my husband died, I went around to different churches asking if they had a ministry to widows. All of them said no. I could not find any programs online to help me either. And that's when I decided to begin Widows Link, to assist churches in starting a small group ministry for widows.

With a vast array of decisions for widows to work through, sometimes it is just easier not to face them. Many choose, as Joann did, to stay within the confines of their home. That is why Widows Link was created: to help widows to get out of their homes and connect with others. We want to provide a support system to help them walk through all the new challenges of this very strange wilderness.

There is such a tremendous need in our world to help widows. In the United States, a woman becomes a widow every forty-five seconds of every day. Yesterday over 1,900 American women stepped into the dark journey of being a widow.

The Lord instructs us to care for widows, and in doing so, we are showing what "genuine religion" really is. James 1:27 (NLT) says, "Pure and genuine religion in the sight of God the Father means caring for orphans and widows." This book is a tool to help you accomplish that.

We pray that your heart has been stirred and that you see the need for this ministry. May this program help you in connecting widows in your community so that together they can find hope, purpose, and the love of Christ as they walk the journey of widowhood, no longer alone.

Testimonial: Pam Bolyard, Widows' Group Leader in Lakeland, Florida

Tony and I were children's pastors at our church when we answered the call to missions. We went overseas, came back, and had a little transition with our kids. Then Tony was diagnosed with colon cancer in 2018. It was an aggressive cancer, and after he died, I walked through two years of real raw grief, with all the struggles and the "where am I?" questions.

When he passed in 2019, God really began to minister to me. In fact, two weeks after Tony passed, I wrote in my journal, "Take widows' ministry to the world."

Unfortunately, I was already discovering that there was nothing in the church designed to support widows and their unique needs. When you have a spouse, you become as one, and when you lose that person, all of a sudden you're like, "Who am I now?" Having a good friend is great, but if she's not a widow, there are important needs you don't have in common.

At first I was apprehensive about getting out, and then when I did get out, I realized how really alone I was. After church no one would ask me out to go eat, so I ate alone; it was a lonely, hard time. I know other widows who feel the same way; they don't want to go out or interact unless they go with a group. You just don't have the confidence like you did before. You don't like doing things alone when you've always done them with someone, when you've always had that person with you.

Then I began to meet other widows and realized they were struggling too. As we found each other, we encouraged each other, and we just felt like sisters because of our shared experiences. We had different challenges than married or single women in the church. We really did need each other.

I was reading in 1 Timothy 5 about how God wants the church to take care of widows. There is a provision in there for family—if family members can take care of a widow, that's what Paul recommends. But there are a lot of widows who either don't have family, don't have family close, or they don't have a Christian family who understand the Bible and the needs of the widow.

This is why supporting widows is such a great ministry for the church. And yet, talking to churches over the last couple of months, I'm realizing many don't seem to understand the importance.

I want to teach the pastors and their wives about the importance of widows' ministry. I was able to get in touch with Marlene Craft, and she sat down with me and taught me how to begin a small group ministry to widows. So with my pastor's approval we started a widows' ministry at our church. We launched it with a fall banquet. We wanted to communicate to the widows in our church, "You are important. We are going to take time for you, we are going to give you gifts, we're going to acknowledge you and hug you, we are going to communicate that you're important to us."

Then we began meeting once a month for regular meetings, and once a month we all go out to eat together. Now we're trying to plan outings using some of the suggestions from this program itself. We have to be thoughtful about where we go so that everyone can be involved, often going to the museum for the day or somewhere similar. The ladies were really excited as we talked about taking these short day trips. We took a trip down to Sarasota to an Amish restaurant. It was a really good bonding experience. We got to talk about the struggles they were going through, more so than during any other trip we've ever taken. We really enjoyed that.

One widow is somewhat housebound; she doesn't have anybody that takes her out much. She really looks forward to our meetings. She'll come early to help; she'll ask me to pick her up so she can spend time talking and spend more time out. I think that's helped her a lot in being a part of the group.

I have noticed that some of the widows have gained more confidence in themselves since we began meeting. They feel more secure because they are now part of something in our church, part of a group. And it gives them confidence and security.

When you have your husband, he's like your best friend. You call him, share your day and other details of your life, and if your car breaks down, you can call him. As I have gotten to know these widows, I know that I can count on them if I need help or am having a bad day. We have created a prayer chain for each other and our families. We text each other our prayer requests. It's been a year now since we've started this, and we've really grown and can count on each other.

Relationship building is God's design—all elements in the kingdom are based in relationships. I think that's a crucial part of widows' ministry, to be able to help widows form new relationships. In fact, we're doing our outreach next month to the community for the widows and the widowers who have lost a spouse. We're excited about that, and I told them they're all involved. I have taught them that part of healing is reaching out to others. They will bring food, come fellowship, and invite people to participate. It gives them a purpose for their life. I think that's an important factor, and that is what having a small group ministry to widows can help them with.

It is now my joy to work with Marlene Craft and be a part of the Widows Link team, as we help churches in beginning a widows' ministry.

CHAPTER 2

THE CHALLENGES OF WIDOWHOOD

Let's take a closer look at some of the issues widows face so we can better understand the needs to be addressed in a ministry to widows.

Understanding the Pain

Losing your spouse can be the most stressful event in one's life. When two become one, especially over decades of time, there is much pain in the final separation from your mate. Marriage is like most other things in life, where routines and patterns form. It's just the way life is . . . until one day when your world gets turned upside down. In a moment, everything changes. He's not there. There's no one sleeping next to you. You're not making breakfast or dinner for him anymore. No one is there each night to share the events of your day.

In the movie *Shall We Dance*, the wife explains to the detective the reason people get married. She says, "Because we need a witness for our life. In a world of millions of people, marriage says, 'Your life will not go unnoticed because I will be your witness.'"[2] After a spouse passes away, the remaining spouse no longer has someone to witness their life, to share each day with.

Most married people never stop to consider life as a widow or widower. If thoughts of a spouse's death ever enter our minds, we tend to push them away. This is unfortunate because the death of a spouse is a reality that will impact almost every marriage.

Understanding the Reality of Widowhood

One spouse will more than likely die first, and 80 percent of the time it is the man who dies first. On average, 1,900 women become widows each day in the United States.[3] To put that in perspective, every single morning you wake up, 1,900 ladies are waking up to a life forever changed because her lover and best friend is gone. Who is reaching out to these women? Who will walk them through this?

- Death of a spouse is ranked as the number one stress factor in a person's life.[4]
- There are over fifteen million widows and widowers in the United States. Over eleven million of them are women.[5]
- Nearly 700,000 women lose their husbands each year and will be widows for an average of fourteen years.[6]
- Over 14 percent of widows over the age of sixty-five have incomes below the poverty threshold.[7]
- When we take a look at the statistics, it is a wake-up call for the church to take time to look across our communities. We will find that widows are all around us, and it is not an easy road to adjust to alone. And the numbers are only increasing as people are living longer.

Loneliness

Family, friends, and the church are wonderful comforters to have around after a spouse dies. However, after a few weeks, the visits stop, the phone calls diminish, and sympathy cards have ceased. Everyone else has gone on with their life, but the widow is still grieving the death of her helpmate.

Loneliness threatens to overwhelm each widow as the storm of emotions, questions, and fears surround her. Her kids don't understand what she is going through; they've lost a father, while the widow has lost her partner in life. Friends aren't quite sure what to say because they still have their spouse. Those friendships may also seem to slip slowly away. Even those within the church struggle with knowing what to say. For some, it is easier to just turn away and not say anything. Widows lose the vast majority of their friends after their spouse dies.

Many widows find themselves alone at home all day with no one to talk to. Some still have jobs or end up needing to find a job to support themselves. Even if they find satisfaction in work, they still come home to an empty house. Going out can be hard on a widow as well. Whether it is a restaurant or a movie, couples are everywhere you look.

One of the biggest challenges for widows is going to bed at night. Some widows can't sleep in their bed, so they find a different bed or try to find rest in their husband's recliner. After years of sleeping next to their best friend, now each night is a reminder of what they no longer have.

Doing Things By Herself

Another new reality widows must face is how many things their spouse took care of. Now they have to take care of these tasks or figure out a way to get them done. For example, a home is always needing repairs. For many women, the first time they have to take out the trash is hard. "This was my husband's job." The car is a whole challenge in itself. Most of us don't know enough about our vehicles, from how to check the fluids to how to change the oil. For some widows, it's even a new challenge to fill up the car with gas. Who can we trust to help us with our vehicle?

When it comes to making decisions, there had always been two people involved. Now widows are having to make decisions alone. It used to be so helpful to hear the other side. Aren't two heads better than one? Where is that balance now? How can a widow trust herself? Her husband was her confidant. Who will she trust with financial decisions now that he's gone?

Without a husband sitting across the table to discuss these life challenges, where does the widow turn? Widows need relationships with those who can relate to and understand the wide array of challenges ahead. What every widow needs is a community of ladies who have walked the path and can be there to understand and encourage her. They need a community they can trust. Those who have traveled a similar path can provide a safe environment of healing and restoration and a path through the dense forest of widowhood. These connections are able to give hope for the future.

So here stands the widow, facing a whole new reality of life, where even selfies are another reminder of being alone. There is a void that very few can understand. She has a deep longing for connection within a safe relationship. This is where God's church needs to step in and connect widows to one another. James 1:27 (NLT) tells us that "pure and genuine religion" is "caring for orphans and widows." This guide aims to equip the church to fulfill God's command by connecting widows together, helping them discover their divine design, and empowering them to live out the rest of their lives with purpose and passion.

Let's take a look at some of the scriptures that give us God's perspective on widows and our responsibilities to them.

What the Bible Says About Widows

The Bible clearly tells us our responsibility is to care for widows. The foundation of any ministry should be based on the Word of God. There are over 120 verses in the Bible that talk about widows. Below are some of the verses referring to widows:

James 1:27 (NLT) — *Pure and genuine religion in the sight of God the Father means caring for orphans and widows in their distress and refusing to let the world corrupt you.*

Isaiah 1:17 (NLT) — *Learn to do good. Seek justice. Help the oppressed. Defend the cause of orphans. Fight for the rights of widows.*

Psalms 146:9 (NLT) — *The LORD protects the foreigners among us. He cares for the orphans and widows, but he frustrates the plans of the wicked.*

Exodus 22:22–24 (NIV) — *Do not take advantage of the widow or the fatherless. If you do and they cry out to me, I will certainly hear their cry. My anger will be aroused, and I will kill you with the sword; your wives will become widows and your children fatherless.*

Psalms 68:5 (NIV) — *A father to the fatherless, a defender of widows, is God in his holy dwelling.*

Deuteronomy 14:28–29 (NIV) — *At the end of every three years, bring all the tithes of that year's produce and store it in your towns, so that the Levites (who have no allotment or inheritance of their own) and the foreigners, the fatherless and the widows who live in your towns may come and eat and be satisfied, and so that the LORD your God may bless you in all the work of your hands.*

Deuteronomy 10:18 (NIV) — *He (The Lord God) defends the cause of the fatherless and the widow.*

Deuteronomy 16:14 (NLT) — *This festival will be a happy time of celebrating with your sons and daughters, your male and female servants, and the Levites, foreigners, orphans, and widows from your towns.*

Deuteronomy 24:17 (NLT) — *True justice must be given to foreigners living among you and to orphans, and you must never accept a widow's garment as security for her debt.*

Isaiah 10:1–2 (NLT) — *What sorrow awaits the unjust judges and those who issue unfair laws. They deprive the poor of justice and deny the rights of the needy among my people. They prey on widows and take advantage of orphans.*

Mark 12:43–44 (NLT) — *Jesus called his disciples to him and said, "I tell you the truth, this poor widow has given more than all the others who are making contributions. For they gave a tiny part of their surplus, but she, poor as she is, has given everything she had to live on."*

(See also Acts 6:1–7 and 1 Timothy 5:3–16.)

Testimonial: Jennifer Presley, Pastor's Wife in Ozark, Alabama

My husband and I have been in ministry for twenty-five years, pastoring for the last twenty years. As a pastor's wife, you might think that I would have been aware of widows' needs, but actually I was not. It was not until my grandmother became a widow that my eyes were opened to a widow's journey. She wasn't in my church, but in talking with her, I began to see her many needs. My eyes really opened when Marlene Craft came to our church to share about widows' ministry. The Lord brought my grandmother's experience back to my mind. I began thinking that we really need to start looking at who we have in our church. It was then that the Lord awakened me, as I listened to Marlene's heart and heard about the ministry we could have to widows. I began seeing all the widows in our church who needed to be connected.

In ministry, I have seen a lot of widows withdraw into themselves. Many really want to connect with other people; yet they feel they need to stay guarded. They would have needs around their homes, repairs and those kinds of things, that they would not tell anyone about. I also noticed that our older widows didn't seem to connect with other non-widowed women in any way. They weren't showing up at our women's events, typically because the meetings were at nighttime and many of them didn't want to drive at night.

Especially at the church we're at now, I'm trying to see all the ladies who aren't a part of any kind of women's event and say, "Okay, why are they not a part of things?" I noticed that there was a large group of older widows, so that's where we started. They just wanted to be connected, so what can we do to help them get connected? They were lonely, and if they had a prayer need, they didn't want to bother me, yet I could tell they wanted somebody to talk to. We started trying to figure out how we could connect these women to other women in our church, even during the daytime so they wouldn't have to travel at night.

Many of these widows have been part of the church for a long time. Widows seem to close up; they don't want to bother anyone. Some widows have a hard time coming back to church. Many of their memories with their husbands are associated with being in church. I am currently seeing some widows who feel overwhelmed with emotions, and they don't want to express that in front of everyone, so they stay away from church gatherings and social events. We try to encourage them by saying, "We still need you here; you're a part of this church. We love you and miss you when you're not here. We will do what we can to help you."

It can be challenging to understand what they are going through because I have not experienced it. I try to be sensitive to where they are in their journey. I have found that if I will just start a conversation about what they are wearing or just something random to let them know that I am interested in what they have to say, then they will sit there and talk away. I rely on the Holy Spirit to help me to ask some good questions to let them know I care. Many do want to share about their spouse, and I love to listen to them.

I found that many people tend to shy away from widows because they don't know what to say. I used to be that way myself. I didn't want to say something that would make them cry. But over the last year and a half as I have spent time with these ladies, I have found that many of them just want to talk; they want to be loved on. Open the conversation and allow them to tell you what they want to express. Sometimes we laugh together—actually we laugh a lot! Sometimes we cry together; we may be sitting in a restaurant, but that's okay. We just sit and love on one another and let each other talk as much as we want to talk.

As we have begun using the Widows Link program here at our church, it has been awesome to watch the ladies at their meetings. I watch them talking and sharing with one another. They can relate to each other; they are able to share memories and reminisce with their group. I can tell it really helps them; the smiles on their faces communicate that.

Sometimes we meet at a local restaurant and the widows sit and eat together. We even have other widows from the community join us. It has been awesome to watch because our widows are inviting their other friends who are also widows. Some widows come to meetings who don't go to church at all.

At our former church, we began with a widows' banquet as the program suggests, and then we started our small group widows' ministry. When we moved to our new church, one day while I was unpacking and getting settled into my office, I came across the widows' ministry folder. I asked the Lord if He wanted me to begin one at our new church and to give me confirmation. Within two days I had a widow come to me and say, "I feel like the Lord laid it on my heart to begin a widows' ministry." There was my confirmation! We started meeting over lunch every other Wednesday. Five months later we had our first banquet, which has now become an annual event.

As pastors we pray and talk and counsel a lot of people. Having a widows' ministry provides these widows an opportunity to chat with other widows, and they will call one another throughout the week.

Some of the widows are now gathering in groups to play Dominoes and Scrabble.

Almost every time we meet, I hear a widow talk about how very lonely she is. I also hear, "I don't have anyone come visit me, nobody calls. All the people I used to be friends with are still friends, we see each other, but there's no connection there." So coming together as widows regularly has helped meet their need for one-on-one relationships.

I would suggest to church people to take time to connect with the widows in their church. They are like a treasure box full of so much wisdom. They have giftings that the Lord gave them, so help them find a way to use those gifts. Many times, all it takes is asking them to help in doing something very small. Let them do these small things, especially if you have some tasks that they can do sitting down (if they're older). For example, many of our widows come to wrap presents for teenage kids for Christmas. Just give them an opportunity to serve, no matter how small and insignificant you think it might be. Let them be a part of serving others and it will help keep them connected to the church and with the congregation.

Proverbs 17:22 (NKJV) says, "A merry heart does good, like medicine, but a broken spirit dries the bones." We want to love on our widows. Just because their spouse has passed away doesn't mean they don't have value. We want to do all that we can to continue loving them, where they will feel like they are a valuable part of the body of Christ.

Many widows feel forgotten. My goal, with the Lord's help, is to love on them, but first to give them a place to talk, to laugh, and to cry.

CHAPTER 3

GETTING APPROVAL TO START A MINISTRY TO WIDOWS

After a lot of prayer and reading over this program, one of the first things you want to do is to set up an appointment to speak with your pastor or the person overseeing the ministries at your church—such as the small group, women's, or senior adult ministry leader.

You will want to share your heart for wanting to begin a ministry to widows. For some of you, maybe it was the pastor who approached you about starting a widows' ministry. If your pastor is not familiar with this program, share your ideas of how you would like to begin and the plans you have for the future. Having the support of those in authority is very important to the success of the ministry.

Have a suggested date that you would like to begin. Communicate with the correct person to see if your date will work, considering other church events. If you plan on meeting at the church, you will want to check to make sure the facility, room, or space you want to use is available for the date you are considering.

Whether you are beginning with a banquet or starting off with regular meetings, give the pastor the plans you have for the first several months. Too often the church has seen ministries or groups begin, only to fall flat a short while later. So think ahead and share your plans with the pastor. You will want to get his approval and blessing for this ministry.

Some of you may be thinking about the cost of beginning this. Money is not a necessity for starting a ministry to widows. Many groups have found that once they begin the ministry, the church sees the importance and will add the ministry to their yearly budget. If your church is able to budget some money to help the ministry, it can aid in expenses, such as postage, refreshments, gifts, and possibly child care, among other costs.

If you plan to begin the ministry with a banquet, approach the church about assisting with the cost of the food. There are several options if the church cannot provide those funds. You will find those in the banquet outline.

Some widows' groups have begun with no financial help, and as the ministry grew, the church then added it to their budget. Our prayer is that the church will see God's call to care for widows and will join hands to help in whatever way they can.

Your church may approach you about how much money you will need yearly. Here are a couple of ideas regarding a proposed budget.

1. If there are twenty widows in your group, consider a proposed annual budget of $50 per widow. This would be an annual budget of $1,000. You could expand or reduce it according to the financial status of the church.

2. Using the same annual $1,000 budget, you can break it down into categories:

Cards and Stamps	$100.00
Flowers	$100.00
Banquet	$400.00
Gifts	$300.00
Transportation for events	$100.00

You may also want to consider a budget item for an Emergency/ Discretionary Fund.

Some churches take a one-dollar offering quarterly, specifically for the budget of ministry to widows. Remember that the lack of finances should not deter ministering to widows. The Lord will provide as you step out in faith to reach these precious ladies.

Testimonial: Liz Whisenant, U3B Church in Gadsden, Alabama

My husband and I attend U3B Church in Gadsden, Alabama. When the Lord first laid it on my heart to minister to widows, I thought it was strange because I had never been a widow. At first I said, "No, no, no," but as I continued to pray about it, finally I told the Lord, "Well, if You want me to do it, I will."

I searched the internet trying to find some guidance on how to do a widows' ministry. Then I came across the Widows Link website, and while checking it out, I discovered two videos where Marlene Craft explained how to begin a widows' ministry. So I went to my pastor and shared with him what God had told me to do and that through watching the videos had learned how to begin a widows' ministry. My pastor checked out the website and videos and got back with me. He said, "If God told you to do it, you need to start it."

When I contacted Marlene, she sent the two chapters from the program that went along with the videos. I felt like now everything was laid out in those pages so I could have my ducks in a row. I thought that our church had about four widows, but as I began planning for the kickoff event, I was surprised to find there were twelve widows in our church! It gave me such joy knowing that God was using me to minister to these ladies by connecting them together.

As I began the planning for the banquet, I made sure to keep the pastor updated on what they were doing. People of the church found out what I was planning, and before I knew it there were ten people who came alongside to help put it all together. Many gave money toward the project, and we were able to buy several new items, including chair covers, tablecloths, and even new dishes. They wanted everything new to convey to those ladies how important they were.

The day of the kickoff went so smoothly. The widows had a wonderful time as they enjoyed games and a speaker, yet most of all, I watched as they talked and shared with one another.

After the kickoff event, I began to have regular monthly meetings. Now when our group goes somewhere together, the church pays for the gas. At the church's next business meeting, everything will become official, and the widows' group will be considered an official ministry of the church and will be included in the yearly church budget.

Presently, U3B church is the only church in the community that has a widows' ministry. Since it's a smaller town, word of mouth helped spread the news about what I've been doing. Already another church has contacted me about beginning a widows' ministry for the ladies in their area. My desire is that as other churches begin widows' ministries, we can all come together to put on larger events.

I wanted to share one story that is very special to me . . .

We have one lady who is very shy; I really didn't even know she was a widow. We went on a trip to the children's home, and she almost backed out, but she ended up going. On the way to the children's home the ladies were laughing and cutting up, just talking about different things: shoes, clothes, you know, just whatever.

But on the way home, it was a whole different story since they had spent a couple of days together. It was a different atmosphere. They were sharing about things that normally you wouldn't talk about. Spending that time together helped them to connect in a special way.

No one wants to be complaining about stuff all the time, but sometimes you need to talk about your hurts and your pains; it's not just about being smiley and happy all the time. I could see how much these ladies really needed each other. All it took was me saying, "Lord, I will do it."

CHAPTER 4

PLANNING
THE KICKOFF EVENT

One of the best ways to introduce your new ministry is by first honoring the widows in your church and community. You can do this by having a kickoff event such as a banquet, luncheon, or even a simple tea; this will help you connect with your local widows.

This also gives you an avenue to invite widows from your church, from surrounding churches, and from the community as a whole. Many times, there are not many widows within a church, so they get looked over. This is a wonderful opportunity to bring together the family of God while reaching out to your community. After the banquet you can then begin regular meetings.

Some churches have decided to continue to have a yearly banquet. It is a great opportunity to bring in new widows from the surrounding area.

If it is not possible for your church to begin with a luncheon or banquet, that is not a problem. Go on to the next chapter which explains how to begin your meetings. When the time is right, you can plan a special banquet to honor the widows.

Now, let's get started with planning the kickoff event. The information on the following pages includes many ideas to help you. Pick and choose the ones that work best for your community. You can always add more pieces each year.

First, decide if you will have a banquet, luncheon, or a simple tea. A banquet is where the ladies are served. Many times a luncheon is set up where the widows go through a line to get their food. A tea is simply beverages with cookies or pastries. You can title and tailor your event to whatever best fits your church or community.

Below are several ideas to help in the planning of your kickoff event. The ideas are set up in a simplified outline form and can be used as a checklist.

BEFORE THE KICKOFF EVENT

1. Decide on a location.
2. Choose possible dates and times for the event:
   A. Have several possible dates in case your first choice is unavailable.
   B. Keep in mind many widows have trouble driving at night.
3. Food:
   A. Menu
   B. Who will cook
      1) Church paying for the food
      2) Women of the church making the dishes
      3) Church people bringing potluck meals
   C. Cost
4. Decide whether you will have a speaker, singer, program, games:

      A. Cost/accommodations/transportation

      B. Sound system/podium

5. Decorations:

      A. Theme

      B. Tableware

      C. Name tags—*very* important!

      If they RSVP, you can make name tags ahead of time.

6. Publicity:

      A. Flyers

          1) It is good to convey in the flyer that widows are being honored.

          2) Include place, date, time, RSVP with phone number.

          3) Dress (casual works well and is all-inclusive).

          4) Provide a contact number.

          5) Consider offering transportation if someone needs it.

          6) I would advise to have it for women only.

             Inviting widowers can add tension to the event. You want the widows to relax and enjoy themselves.

          7) You can have an online registration form for them to fill out, but keep in mind that many senior widows are not tech savvy.

      B. Bring the flyers to several locations:

          1) Senior centers

          2) Retirement villages

          3) Other churches

          4) YMCA

          5) Grocery stores

          6) Pharmacies and doctors' offices

    C. Social Media—if you need help, enlist someone from your church to assist you.

    D. News Releases—newspaper, radio stations, senior magazines

    E. Contact your local paper; they may come out and take pictures for an article.

    F. Personal Invitations

    G. Have widows sign up by phone call or email or on your church website.

7. Volunteers—Involve the church!

   This is a way that Christians can obey James 1:27.

    A. Greeters—Have several! These are people who love to hug and love on people and to give directions, i.e., which way to go for the event, along with restroom locations. Having someone opening the door is always helpful. Having a red carpet down the hallway as they come in makes them feel special.

    B. Servers—These can be deacons, elders, youth, couples, scouts, etc.

    C. Valet parkers—Consider making valet parking an option.

    D. Setup crew

    E. Photographer

    F. Sound person

    G. Cleanup crew

    H. It is a good idea to plan to feed your volunteers, i.e., either the banquet food or pizza.

8. Door prizes and/or gifts and flowers at the table:

    A. This is an important part because widows miss getting gifts and flowers.

    B. Door prizes can be gathered from around the community. Churches have found that businesses love the idea of helping widows.

    C. Gifts at the table can be anything, whether homemade or small store-bought gifts. It is best not to have used items as gifts.

    D. Flowers are always a nice touch. They can be used as centerpieces and even sent home with the widows as prizes or gifts.

9.   Make a list of the order of your service/banquet.
    Having a written program for yourself and those who are helping. It will help to keep you on track.

Remember that not all banquets will look the same. You should put the banquet together as it best fits your church and community. As you work together, you are fulfilling God's command to care for widows. Your main purpose is to bring widows together, to honor, uplift, and love them in Christ.

DURING THE KICKOFF EVENT

1.   Collect key information on widows.
    A. In chapter 7, "Widows Link Program Resources," you will find two different "Widow Information Sheets." Here is an explanation of how to use them:
      1) The form called "Widow Information Sheet A" can be used if you have not yet decided on a definite time for your regular meetings. The ladies' answers to questions 1 and 2 on this sheet will give you the best times for the widows.

    2) The form called "Widow Information Sheet B" (2 per page) can be used if you have already set the day and time for the regular widows' small group meetings. These sheets can also be used when you have visitors at your regular meetings. Getting visitors' information helps in following up with them.

    B. Some churches have the widows write their addresses on an envelope so they can send them an invitation to next year's banquet. This would be in addition to getting their information sheets.

2.   Play one or two games, or icebreakers, to get the women talking to one another. This helps to create a fun, relaxing atmosphere. Another option is to have "conversation starters" written on cards on the table. In chapter 7 you'll find a list of conversation starters.

3.   Speaker:

   A. Comedian

   B. Widow with a special and uplifting testimony

   C. Widows sharing funny stories or sayings

   D. Band

    One church had a band and the ladies danced to the oldies.

4.   Gifts/Flowers (feel free to choose one or more of these ideas):

   A. Give a flower, either real or fake, to each widow.

    One church gave fake roses with this quote on a slip of paper attached: "The Lord's love will never fade away."

   B. A small gift, such as an encouraging plaque, candle, scented hand soap, or stationery.

   C. Door prizes are fun.

Tickets are simple to use. They can be found now at Dollar Tree and Walmart.

    D. Candy, especially chocolate, is always a nice treat. *Involve a group in your church to bag the candy in a decorative way.*

    E. Make sure every widow goes home with some sort of gift. (If you only do a few larger prizes, make sure everyone has something special to take home.)

5. Things on the table (as a reminder):

    A. Widow Information Sheet

    B. Pens

    C. Game Sheets

    D. Announcement of next meeting

    If you are able to plan your first regular widows' small group meeting, then have a reminder notice printed for them so they can put it on their refrigerator.

6. Pictures:

    A. You can set up a "picture area" with a nice background setting. Possibly have a volunteer at the photo booth to take the ladies' pictures.

    B. One church had a photographer who took individual pictures of the widows as they arrived, then went to have them developed, and handed them out at the end of the banquet.

    C. Widows don't usually think about having a nice picture of themselves.

7. Time/length of the event:

    Keep the length of the event between one to two hours.

8. Departure/end of the event:

A. As the widows are leaving, again hug them and thank them for coming; this is part of showing them Christ's love.

B. Make sure to gather all the Widow Information Sheets from the tables. This information will help you in planning future meetings for the widows.

AFTER THE KICKOFF EVENT

Within a week after the kickoff event, send a thank-you note to those team members who helped with your event. We don't do this ministry alone, so it's important always to have a grateful heart. Also, when you need help in the future, you will find it easier to get those same people to lend a hand.

Here are some suggestions on how to use the Widow Information Sheets:

1. Get a binder to keep all the sheets together.

2. If you have not yet decided on the time and date for your small group meetings, look over the Widow Information Sheet A. The answers to questions 1 and 2 will help you in deciding a good time to meet and how often.
   Check with the pastor or person in authority at your church regarding the date you will set for the first small group meeting. Have a first and second choice for meeting times when you talk with this leader to get their approval. Another option is to discuss at your first small group meeting whether or not the chosen time is agreed upon by the majority. Usually those who attend your first meeting will be the ones who will be coming regularly.

3. Use the answers to questions 3 and 4 to make a list of ideas for things to do and places to go. Keep that list in the front of your binder for future reference.

4. Look at question 5 and see if there are any immediate needs that should be addressed.

    A. You can talk with your pastor or person in authority to get some help and guidance in meeting these needs.

    B. Some churches have a point man for widows to contact if they have some needs around their house.

5. Other suggestions for using the Widow Information Sheets:

    A. You can write thank-you notes to the widows who attended the event and tell them about your upcoming meeting.

    B. Putting all the widows' information on a spreadsheet can be helpful if you have someone who could do that. For some people, paper works better than a spreadsheet.

    C. Get a calendar and put all the important dates from the Widow Information Sheets on it. This will help you or someone in your group in sending birthday cards and notes of encouragement.

One final suggestion after the kickoff event would be to have your team members do an evaluation of the event. Hand out the "Banquet/Kickoff Evaluation Form" (located in chapter 7, "Resources") to each of your team members, asking them to fill it out the same day or within the next few days following your event. Then, as a group, look them over and see how you can make your future banquets better.

Testimonial: Pastor Bill Bryan, The Bridge Church, Cusseta, Alabama

Our church is in a rural community in the middle of cow pastures with a college town about thirty miles away. In 2015 we had an unusual number of deaths, resulting in quite a few widows. As I began to look around the church, I noticed there were more widows than we had realized. Our church was challenged by the verse in James of how real religion or real relationship with Father God is taking care of widows and orphans. And even though it was a command, it seemed like not many churches were doing much to follow that command, and our church was not doing that much to help widows either. Then we found out that Marlene Craft had become the first missionary to widows in her denomination, so we got in touch with her.

Marlene met with me and shared an outline of how to begin a widows' ministry. She suggested we begin with a widows' banquet, inviting the widows of the community and feeding them, loving on them, and letting them know that Christ loves them too.

We took her outline and got a team together and began to go over the list. Being in a rural community, surrounded by three other towns, we came up with ideas that would best serve our widows. As I shared the vision with the church, everyone loved the idea. It was the easiest thing we have ever done in the thirty years of serving at this church.

With all the excitement about the kickoff event, all departments got involved. The kids handed out flowers, teenagers escorted the ladies in, the men of the church provided valet parking, and the women were involved in cooking and serving. We continue to do the banquets yearly, and it is probably the most fun event we do now each year. I would like other pastors to know that if you give your people an opportunity, this event will be one of your best events of the year.

We have learned that one of the most important parts is doing any advertising you can, along with word of mouth. Our church did a lot of Facebook advertising and realized that most newspapers will do something like this for free. Now after seven years of doing these yearly banquets, we send out sixty letters to all the surrounding churches in the area inviting their widows to come to the event. It is an event for the region. We reassure them that this is not a proselytizing thing.

We keep a list of everyone who comes and then send out invitations the following year, inviting them to come back. Also we try to call each woman a week before the banquet. I feel the excitement begins with the invitation, and then getting a personal phone call adds to the anticipation. When the widows arrive, they can feel the love. The workers have seen dispositions change as the ladies walk into the banquet. For many widows who may not have family around or who don't have children, this is a day of hope. We've watched some come in sad and leave on cloud nine. The church's motto for that day is "Treat them like the queens they are."

After our first banquet, as we saw the joy, the laughter, and the peace on the faces of those widows, we as a church decided that this would become an annual event. We choose to do their banquets around Valentine's Day because it is one of the hardest days of the year for widows. Our church also used the first banquet to share with all the widows that we were beginning a monthly get-together for them. We shared the next two months' meeting dates and gave the ladies a reminder flyer.

Out here in cow country, over the past eight years we have grown from the thirty we had the first year to over eighty widows coming from all over the area. This past year, in the midst of closing prayer time, a couple of widows asked Jesus into their hearts. The banquets are an opportunity for our church to love on the widows as God has commanded us, and it is also a time when the Lord can touch their hearts."

The part I enjoy the most is the change of frowns turning into smiles, the frowns of someone who came in, maybe a little reluctant. And suddenly, they're opening up, they're singing, they're laughing, they're meeting people, they're enjoying the food.

Through all the years we have been doing these banquets, I don't know of a widow who has ever walked away the same. So I think that's probably the greatest testimony you can have, that everyone is being affected by what you're doing on that one day. I mean, so many Sundays come and go, and not everyone sees a lot of change, but we have a banquet or a widows' meeting, and I believe there's a lot of change every time they get together.

For those who are thinking about starting a widows' ministry, consider this: if we are not reaching them, we would have to ask ourselves, do we really want to obey the commands of the Lord in reaching them? So, we have to have that heart, or develop that heart.

Something I pray almost every day is for God to help me to see people as God sees them, and we know that He has a special place in his eyes for widows. He's definitely a husband to those who don't have husbands.

My biggest advice is just start somewhere. I mean, even if you only have three widows, take them out for dinner with your husband or wife or take them out yourself.

Anytime you do something new, there's always a fear of failure, but there is no failure when you're reaching out to widows in any way, shape, or form.

So just start, just start somewhere. But even if you don't have the money to do it, just start with a meal with just you and your widows and then invite them to bring a friend once a month. If you're only reaching two of them, you're still obeying what the Lord says to do, so that's the most important part.

CHAPTER 5

STARTING
THE SMALL GROUP MEETINGS

Anyone can lead a widows' ministry. You don't have to be a widow. I've seen wonderful widows' ministries that have been led by couples and even singles. The important thing is that you have a heart for widows. The Lord has called us to be a body working together, so ask the Lord to give you others to work with you in this ministry.

IF YOU CHOOSE NOT TO HAVE A KICKOFF EVENT

For those who do not begin with a kickoff event, you can have the widows fill out the Widow Information Sheet A before your first meeting so you can use their answers in planning the first meetings. There is also the option to have them fill it out at the first meeting and then decide on the details for future meetings according to the answers on the sheets.

USING THE WIDOW INFORMATION SHEETS

Set a time when the team can meet together to look over the Widow Information Sheets. From the sheets you can decide the following:

- How often your group will meet
- What day of the week your group will meet
- What time will work best for your group to meet

Every church and community is different. How often you meet is for you to decide. The vision of Widows Link is to connect widows. Keep in mind that widows need to talk with each other because it helps in their healing.

Realize you can always change the times you meet down the road if you want. Our first few years we met twice a month. When my traveling increased and the new leader took over, she changed it to once a month. Listen and be sensitive to what group members would like. Remember, though, that you won't be able to make everyone happy all the time.

If you are beginning this ministry alone, go forward and keep believing that the Lord will bring people to walk alongside you. As you are faithful to the Lord, He will honor your work.

PLANNING THE FIRST MEETING

After you have decided the day of the week, time, and frequency of meetings, you can decide on the date of your first meeting. Always check with the church calendar first so you can make sure there will be no conflict with the date, time, and location you've chosen.

LOCATION

There is a lot of flexibility here. The church is an easy place to begin. Other options include places outside the church that may be more "visitor friendly" for non-Christians or widows who attend other denominations—like a library, a coffee shop, a bank, a home, a clubhouse, or a senior center. It helps to keep the same location when you first begin your widows' ministry so the ladies will know where to go.

WHO IS INVITED

We recommend that you limit it to women and not include widowers in the meeting. If your church does have a group of widowers, this program will work for them also. The two groups can meet at separate places and times.

Insofar as including divorcees and singles in your group, that choice is your own. It is true they don't have a male covering, but their journeys are different from the widow's. Let the Lord guide you in this.

THE REASON FOR THE SMALL GROUP MEETINGS

It is important to remember that these meetings are an opportunity for the ladies to open up and get to know one another. You want to create a safe, loving place for the widows to share and to build a family together. Therefore, we encourage you to avoid letting it become "just another Bible study." Widows have a deep need to share what they are feeling and learn from those who have walked the same path.

You can plan things to do at the meetings, but you also want to be flexible and to be led by the Holy Spirit if the women are needing to talk. For the first six months of our small group, I usually put any plans I had made aside so the ladies could share with one another. However, I always included a short devotional and prayer, which we will talk more about in the next section.

THE FORMAT FOR MEETINGS

This is the fun part. The meeting can be whatever you and your group would like it to be. Look over the completed Widow Information Sheets and see what the ladies enjoy and would like to see and do in the widows' ministry. In the following chapter you will find a list of different ideas for your group.

Here are some ideas of things you can do within your meeting:

1. It is nice to have a meeting that includes a meal. Many widows grow weary of eating by themselves. It also helps to create a relaxed atmosphere: eating and sharing, they go together. We see in the Bible how many times Jesus sat and ate with people. Many widows can open up during a meal, more so than just sitting in a group.

   There are a variety of ways to put this together. You can have a potluck meal where everyone brings something or pick up takeout from a restaurant and ask everyone to contribute some money to help pay for it. There may be a Sunday school class or a small group that could help in providing food as well.

2. Decorating the tables helps widows to feel special. If you choose to decorate, you can ask if any of your widows would like to be in charge of decorating the tables for your meetings. The Lord has gifted people in different ways, and some ladies find joy in decorating. It provides an avenue for them to use their talents.

3. Have someone keep attendance or have everyone sign in. Contacting those who were not there lets them know they were missed and are loved.

4. It is important to have name tags. You may think everyone knows each other, yet as visitors come, it is more inviting for them to be able to call someone by their name. And who of us has not forgotten someone's name?

5. Having a short devotional is always good. The Word of God is "a lamp unto [our] feet, and a light unto [our] path" (Psalm 119:105 KJV). Widows need direction in their lives. The Bible encourages and lifts us up and points us and others to Jesus. As we suggested earlier, however, don't make it "just another Bible study." The ladies need to be able to share and talk.

6. Planning some light games (or even having a monthly game day) is a fun option for widows. Games can produce laughter and provide another avenue to get to know each other. Some ladies love a little healthy competition. You can find game ideas on the internet or at your local library.

7. Icebreakers are a great way to get the ladies talking and connecting with each other. These can even end up being the bulk of your meeting, which is fine. Remember the purpose of these small groups is to "connect" the widows together, and icebreakers can do just that. There are hundreds of ideas for icebreakers online.
    Depending on how large your group is, you may want to break it up into smaller groups of six or eight ladies so there is greater opportunity for all to share.

8. In the next chapter, you will find a list of meeting ideas along with outing suggestions. Traveling together, whether it be in a car or van, can be great because it provides time to talk in a smaller group setting. Our small group did

a combination of sometimes having our meetings at the church and other times going somewhere together.

9. You can have a door prize for each of your meetings. Widows miss not getting gifts from their husband. And everyone loves winning prizes! For some people, this can also provide an additional incentive to attend.

10. If you would like some ideas on conversation starters for your meetings, we have a list of questions you can use in chapter 7, "Widows Link Program Resources." You can also read a page or two from a book on grief that would work to get a conversation started about what they have been through or how they are feeling. There is a list of book suggestions also in chapter 7.

11. It is important to be flexible within your meetings. You may have certain plans, but as you watch and listen, you may see that the women just want to talk. Keep in mind you are building family-like connections, and this sharing time allows them to get to know one another on a deeper level.

12. At the end of your meeting, make sure to announce the date of your next meeting. It helps if you can print out reminders or invitations to help them remember once they're home. In many elderly widows' homes you will find upcoming appointments written on notes hanging on their refrigerators. Giving them a tangible reminder will help them to remember the upcoming meeting, even though someone will be calling them to remind them.

Using the Widow Information Sheets, plan on having someone call each group member three to five days before each meeting. You can even send out an invitation for the get-together (invitation samples can be found in chapter 7).

13. Plan a time of prayer during the meeting where widows can pray for one another. Consider that some may not feel comfortable praying out loud or for someone else. You may be able to teach them how to pray for one another. As the disciples said, "Lord, teach us to pray" (Luke 11:1 NIV). Every now and then, have them gather in small groups of two or three to share their requests and then pray for one another.

Caution: you don't want your meetings to become a "Oh, pity me and my problems" time. You want to keep them upbeat. There are times widows definitely need to share their struggles and challenges in widowhood. But you need to ask the Holy Spirit to help you strike a balance; otherwise, some widows will not want to return, as widows face enough down times during their daily lives. As ministry leaders, we are here to listen but also to point them to the hope they have in Jesus.

MORE PLANNING TIPS

Here are a few more ideas on how to make your widows' ministry meetings successful:

1. After holding your first meeting, you should have an idea of how often your group would like to meet and on what days. You've collected the Widow Information Sheets, so you will be able to send them reminders about upcoming meetings and events.

2. Plan the next two meetings so you will have an idea of what things need to be put together before the meetings.

3. As you are planning your different meetings and events, keep in mind that most widows are on a limited income. If every meeting is costing them money, finances could keep them away from joining the group event. Keep costs to widows minimal.

4. Ask someone in your group to make reminder phone calls to the widows a few days before each meeting.

5. See if any of your widows would like to be in charge of decorating the tables for your next meeting or event.

6. Prepare a calendar noting each widow's birthday, special events, etc. Make copies of a monthly calendar to give to each widow. Encourage them to remember each other's birthday. You may want to have all the widows' contact information—their names, addresses, and phone numbers—listed in the front of the calendar.

7. Recruit a team member to help with follow-up for the absentees.

8. Consider giving your small group a name. This creates a sense of belonging. You can ask the ladies to think about some ideas and together make a decision at your next meeting. Having them participate in coming up with a name helps them feel more like part of the group.

Here are some sample names of widows' groups:
  A. W.O.W. (Women of Worth)
  B. Daughters of Ruth
  C. Joy in the Morning
  D. New Beginnings
  E. C.A.M.E.O. (Come and Meet Each Other)

F. Friend Connection

G. Finding Worth in Widowhood

Below are some websites that will give you more ideas of possible names:

A. https://actuallygoodteamnames.com/womens-ministry-names

B. https://groupnamesadda.com/womens-ministry-names

9. The final suggestion is to ask group members to evaluate after the first meeting and then quarterly. Hand out the Meeting Evaluation Forms (located in chapter 7) to your team members. Ask them to fill the form out after the meeting or within a few days following the meeting. As a group, look them over and see how you can improve your meetings.

Now you have the basic format for your meetings. Keep in mind that you want to allow a lot of time for group members to share and talk with one another. Those who have been widowed longer will be able to encourage the newer widows.

Testimonial: Linda Scholtz, Widows' Group Leader in Boone, Colorado

My husband, Paul, and I served as the first rodeo chaplains for the Assemblies of God for almost forty years. He passed away in 2017. Six months after he died, I gathered the widows from my church together for a short weekend getaway. As I watched the ladies sharing with one another, I realized the importance of widows connecting with each other. So I asked the secretary at my home church how many widows they had. The secretary said she had no idea. I exclaimed, "Well, we are going to do something about that."

I asked the pastor if the widows could get together at the church and figure out what they would like to do. Our first meeting was on a Wednesday evening in February of 2020. Then COVID-19 hit! During the shutdown, I was able to spend time with Marlene Craft. Marlene shared all the information on how to do a small group for widows. This really helped because even though I am a widow, I was unsure how to help others.

Marlene's program gave me a basic idea of what to do during widows' small group meetings and things to do to help widows feel special. I have been able to expand the widows' ministry, now leading two different widows' groups.

The widows love having someone who just understands, having someone who's gone through what they've gone through. Several of the other widows and I have made a pact that if we're home, one of us tries be at the funeral of the husband for a new widow, just to be there for them and love on them. We let them know we're here for them. So that begins the connection, and they know someone gets them.

I was reading the part of the chapter about small group meetings that we're not just another Bible study group. So at each meeting, I have a devotion or something that encourages them, but we just give them time to talk.

Some of them are having the one-year anniversary of the death; you just never know who's going through what each week. We just let them have time to share what's going on in in their life, and we all try to encourage and comfort one another. That's what they say they enjoy the most. They just enjoy someone being there, and usually it just comes up on the side: "Well, today would have been our anniversary."

Another lesson I have learned from the program is the importance of having small gifts or door prizes at the meetings. The widows miss getting gifts from their husbands, and many times, even family members do not remember special dates. When Marlene shared with the widows at one of our meetings, Marlene gave Hershey's Kisses to all the widows and talked about how God "kisses" us by blessing us in different ways. It is His way to remind us that He loves us. So I continue to give out Hershey's Kisses at our meetings to remind the ladies to look for those kisses from the Lord.

One special thing I have seen is how the widows bond as sisters. When the ladies call each other or ask for prayer, it is not just about what might be triggering the grief. It's about anything that is going on in their lives. Just like sisters.

The team that we have put together helps to minister to widows who have different kinds of needs. Where my husband had a five-year battle before his death, I am able to minister to those who also went through a long time of knowing their husbands were dying. The other helpers have experienced different types of grief journeys, so they can help other widows. The team tries to make it very encouraging for the new widows, sharing with them hope and a reason to go on.

One other thing that I appreciate is the Widow Information Sheets provided in the program. They were very helpful in gaining a better understanding of our ladies. They were also useful in learning how to design the meetings from the questions on what they liked to do and where they would like to go for meetings and outings. I have also been using some of the resources on the Widows Link website, like the Virtual Widows Conferences. For the group that meets weekly for one hour, I broke down the conference and just showed one speaker a week for four weeks. It worked really well. For my other group for their monthly meeting, I split it up and showed part of the conference in the morning, then had fellowship, ate lunch, and after that we finished watching the rest of the conference in the afternoon.

I am so thankful for this program. It has really helped me to understand how to minister to widows. It has been an incredible tool to help me in walking out what the Lord has put on my heart.

CHAPTER 6

ADDITIONAL MEETING AND OUTREACH IDEAS

One of the most important things about a widows' ministry is connecting widows. As I've emphasized, you want to create an inviting atmosphere where women can relax and share with one another. Below is a list of different things that can be done at or for a meeting. And changing things up occasionally can create excitement and interest. Here are some ideas for you to try:

1. At WidowsLink.org we have a series of videos called "Dear Widow" which address some of the challenges of widowhood. You can use the corresponding discussion questions after watching the videos together at your meetings.

2. Find someone to demonstrate a seasonal art project that you can all do together.

3. Bring someone in to teach for twenty minutes on a relevant topic, such as budgeting, cell phone use, or health-related advice.

4. Dress up and have a tea party.

5. Put together goodie boxes for a specific group of people: soldiers, college students, kids in a children's home or hospital, etc.

6. Make Christmas, holiday, or cheerful cards for people in nursing homes.

7. Bring in a travel agent to come in with pictures and talk about traveling tips.

8. Have a police officer come teach on safety tips.

9. Go to a park or the zoo and have a picnic together.

10. Find free or inexpensive concerts around your community to attend together.

11. Visit a museum or a ballet or a local college theater production.

12. Go to a flower garden, sidewalk art show, or women's conference.

13. Have coloring or puzzles at a meeting or plan a separate day for it.

14. Brainstorm ways you could help single moms.

15. Go to a movie together, then enjoy a sweet treat such as ice cream afterward.

16. Lend a helping hand, together, to other outreach organizations in your community.

17. Go to an art show.

18. Have someone teach on funeral planning, investing, or insurance.

19. Plan or help with a get-together or event for the youth. Cook for them, and have them ask your group questions about your lives.

20. Connect with a local college to see about widows becoming foster grandparents to students.

21. Go to a food shelter and help with organizing or giving out food.

22. Visit shut-ins or residents in a nursing home.

23. Travel together to a tourist attraction in your area.

24. Have a '50s night where you all dress up and make your own sundaes.

25. Contact your local senior center to find more creative ideas of activities to do together.

26. Go on a cruise together.

27. Contact a children's home in your area and see if the widows can come read or play with the kids.

28. Consider doing a book study or book club, preferably on a different day than your regular meetings. There are book suggestions in chapter 7, "Widows Link Program Resources."

29. Consider showing one of our Virtual Widows Conferences (found on our website, WidowsLink.org) during a meeting. Each is approximately seventy-five minutes in length.

30. Consider using one of our Facebook Live presentations at a meeting; we have over eighty of these available on our Facebook page, and they range from ten to twenty minutes.

Have fun and get to know each other through these events. After all, you are building family.

SUMMARY

This is the beginning of great and wonderful things the Lord has in store for you as you step out to reach and support widows in your church or community.

Within this program, you have learned that there is a great need for this ministry and that God has a special place in His heart for widows. You heard examples of women who went through their time of healing surrounded by others who had experienced the loss of their spouse, eventually finding purpose for their lives.

We hope that this program will guide you in helping widows to connect and to discover God's plan for their new journey. Our prayers are with you as you go forward in reaching out to widows. Every soul is important to His kingdom.

Thank you for taking the step forward to make a difference in the lives of these precious women. If we can be of any help, please feel free to contact us on our Connect tab at WidowsLink.org.

May the Lord bless all that your hands do as you reach out to the widows of your community. "Give it to . . . the widows in your towns, so they can eat and be satisfied. Then the LORD your God will bless you in all your work" (Deuteronomy 14:29 NLT).

CHAPTER 7

WIDOWS LINK
PROGRAM RESOURCES

In the following pages you will find many of the resources referenced in earlier chapters. **You can also find digital versions of these resources on our website at: http://widowslink.org/programresources.**

Here is a list of the resources in this chapter:

- Widow Information Sheet A
- Widow Information Sheet B (two per page)
- Sample Kickoff Flyer
- Small Group Meeting Invitations
- Banquet/Kickoff Evaluation Form
- Meeting Evaluation Form
- Conversation Starters
- Book Suggestions
- Suggested Websites and Online Articles
- Frequently Asked Questions

WIDOW INFORMATION SHEET A

Name _____   Birthday _____

Address _____

City _____   State _____   Zip _____

Cell Phone _____   Home Phone _____

Do you text? YES or NO   Do you live alone? YES or NO

Date of Husband's Passing _____

Emergency Contact _____   Phone Number _____

How would you prefer to be contacted? (Circle)   Cell   Home   Text   Email

1.   The best time for you to be involved would be: (mark as many that work)

	Morning	Afternoon	Evening		Morning	Afternoon	Evening
Sunday				Thursday			
Monday				Friday			
Tuesday				Saturday			
Wednesday							

2.   How often would you like to have meetings?

   Weekly _____   Twice a month _____   Monthly _____   Quarterly _____

3.   Do you need transportation to the meetings? YES or NO

4.   What are some activities and hobbies you enjoy? _____

_____

5.   What would you like to see and do in the widows' ministry? _____

_____

6.   Do you have any immediate needs? _____

_____

WIDOW INFORMATION SHEET

Name _____ Birthday _____

Address _____

City _____ State_____ Zip _____

Cell Phone _____ Home Phone _____

Email (please print) _____

Date of Husband's Passing _____ Do you live alone? YES or NO

Emergency Contact _____ Phone Number _____

What are some activities and hobbies you enjoy?

_____

What would you like to see and do in the widows' ministry?

_____

Do you have any immediate needs?

_____

✂ ···

WIDOW INFORMATION SHEET

Name _____ Birthday _____

Address _____

City _____ State_____ Zip _____

Cell Phone _____ Home Phone _____

Email (please print) _____

Date of Husband's Passing _____ Do you live alone? YES or NO

Emergency Contact _____ Phone Number _____

What are some activities and hobbies you enjoy?

_____

What would you like to see and do in the widows' ministry?

_____

Do you have any immediate needs?

_____

Honoring the Widows of Our Community

A Widows Luncheon

(Day and Date)

At (Time of Event)

At (Name of Place)

(Address of location)

(Optional) Sponsored by (Name of Church or Organization)

Fun, Food, And Fellowship

RSVP: (Name and Phone of Contact person)

Special Speaker:

(Name of person)

(Information about speaker.

To the right you can include their picture or a picture that goes with your theme.)

You're Invited to a
Widows' Get-Together

On July 18th at 12 noon
At Smallville Family Church
123 Main St., Smallville
We will enjoy a
Potluck Lunch,
Fun & Fellowship
Invite a Widow Friend
For Questions: Mary at 123-4567

Hope to see you there!

You're Invited to a
Widows' Get-Together

On July 18th at 12 noon
At Smallville Family Church
123 Main St., Smallville
We will enjoy a
Potluck Lunch,
Fun & Fellowship
Invite a Widow Friend
For Questions: Mary at 123-4567

Hope to see you there!

You're Invited to a
Widows' Get-Together

On July 18th at 12 noon
At Smallville Family Church
123 Main St., Smallville
We will enjoy a
Potluck Lunch,
Fun & Fellowship
Invite a Widow Friend
For Questions: Mary at 123-4567

Hope to see you there!

You're Invited to a
Widows' Get-Together

On July 18th at 12 noon
At Smallville Family Church
123 Main St., Smallville
We will enjoy a
Potluck Lunch,
Fun & Fellowship
Invite a Widow Friend
For Questions: Mary at 123-4567

Hope to see you there!

BANQUET/KICKOFF EVALUATION FORM

1. What did you enjoy most about the banquet/kickoff?

   _____

   _____

2. What could have been done in the planning to make the event better?

   _____

   _____

3. Did the speaker communicate effectively?

   _____

   _____

4. Do you feel the time allotted for the banquet was well used?

   _____

   _____

5. What problems came up that may need to be addressed?

   _____

   _____

6. What ideas do you have for future banquets?

   _____

   _____

7. After this event, what are your thoughts about the importance of connecting widows to each other?

   _____

   _____

MEETING EVALUATION FORM

1. What did you enjoy most about the meeting?

    _____

    _____

2. What could have been done in the planning to help make the meeting better?

    _____

    _____

3. Do you feel the time allotted for the meeting was sufficient?

    _____

    _____

4. What problems came up that may need to be addressed?

    _____

    _____

5. What ideas do you have for future meetings?

    _____

    _____

6. Would you like to share a testimony or something special that happened during the meeting?

    _____

    _____

CONVERSATION STARTERS

These are a collection of ideas of things you can discuss at your meetings that will help widows to open up and get to know one another. When using conversation starters, you never want to make it mandatory for everyone to share. In trying to create a safe atmosphere for them, it's best to let them decide when they want to talk. Keep in mind that you do not know what kind of day a widow is having. As we all know, grief is a strange animal and can capture their mind and feelings. Ask the Lord to direct you in what questions to use.

1. What is a funny thing that your husband did?
2. Tell us about how you met your husband.
3. What is a place you would like to visit one day?
4. Who was the most influential person in your life?
5. What has been the hardest part of widowhood so far?
6. Since widowhood, what have you discovered about yourself?
7. What has been the best day of your life so far?
8. Define grief using just three words
9. What is your favorite memory of your husband?
10. What is your favorite verse through grief?
11. What bothers you most about your loss?
12. What is your favorite time of year and why?
13. What is the worst thing that someone has said to you since your loss?
14. What do you wish people around you would understand?
15. Have you ever felt like you just wanted to give up?
16. What is on your bucket list?

17. What are you hopeful about in the future?
18. What do you miss most about your husband?
19. What are you most thankful for during this time of your life?
20. What is one thing you are currently wondering about?
21. What do you fear most about the future?
22. How has grief affected your work at home or at your job?

There are also conversation starter packets you can find online, such as TableTopics.com.

BOOK SUGGESTIONS

For Conversation and Learning

- *Getting to the Other Side of Grief: Overcoming the Loss of a Spouse* by Susan J. Zonnebelt-Smeenge and Robert C. De Vries
- *From One Widow to Another: Conversations on the New You* by Miriam Neff
- *Postcards from the Widows' Path: Gleaning Hope and Purpose from the book of Ruth* by Ferree Hardy
- *Reflections of a Grieving Spouse: The Unexpected Journey from Loss to Renewed Hope* by H. Norman Wright
- *Grieving With Hope: Finding Comfort as You Journey through Loss* by Samuel J. Hodges IV and Kathy Leonard
- *Widow to Widow: Thoughtful, Practical Ideas for Rebuilding Your Life* by Genevieve Davis Ginsburg
- *Not Alone: 11 Inspiring Stories of Courageous Widows from the Bible* by Miriam Neff
- *A Widow's Journey: Reflections on Walking Alone* by Gayle Roper

For Comfort

- *Grace for the Widow: A Journey through the Fog of Loss* by Joyce Rogers
- *Grieving the Loss of Someone You Love: Daily Meditations to Help You through the Grieving Process* by Raymond R. Mitsch and Lynn Brookside

- *The Empty Chair: Handling Grief on Holidays and Special Occasions* by Susan J. Zonnebelt-Smeenge and Robert C. De Vries

For New Widows

- *A Widow's Journey: Reflections on Walking Alone* by Gayle Roper
- *Experiencing Grief* by H. Norman Wright
- *Grace for the Widow: A Journey through the Fog of Loss* by Joyce Rogers
- *Grieving: Your Path Back to Peace* by James R. White

SUGGESTED WEBSITES AND ONLINE ARTICLES

- Widow Connection (www.widowconnection.com)
  Founder: Miriam Neff, author of *From One Widow to Another*

- GriefShare (www.griefshare.org)
  You can sign up for short daily emails of encouragement, free for a year.

- Widow Might (www.widowmight.org)
  Cofounders: David Thielman and Ginger Ewing

- Courage in Grief (https://lp.billygraham.org/courage-in-grief)
  Resource by Billy Graham Evangelistic Association

- Walking Forward (https://walkingforward.org)
  Founder: Miriam Testasecca

- Wings for Widows (www.wingsforwidows.org)
  Free financial counseling for widows

- The Widow's Guide by Prestonwood Baptist Church (https://prestonwood.org/give/foundation/widows-guide/)

- Social Security Survivors Benefits (To apply for benefits: https://www.ssa.gov/pubs/EN-05-10084.pdf

- AARP (https://www.aarp.org/caregiving/basics/info-2017/truth-about-grief.htmlAARP.org/)

FREQUENTLY ASKED QUESTIONS

Q: What should I do if I have a couple of strong people who seem to be controlling the group conversation?

A: Here are a couple of thoughts: When you see that someone is dominating the conversation, look for the right time to cut in and say something complementary. Feel free to comment on what they have shared and then turn to the others and say, "What do you ladies have to share with us?" This gives you a way to politely redirect the conversation to others in the room. Rely on the Holy Spirit to help you with leading the group. Most of the time you will find the ladies love sharing and hearing from each other. They will encourage one another because they understand what the others are going through.

Q: There are some divorcees who lost their husbands. Would they not be considered a widow?

A. There is a difference in their journeys. Though divorcees do go through a grief process, they may have a harder time understanding the deep hole that widows have after their husbands die. The choice is yours whether to include them in your widows' group.

Q. What are some other ways that the church can minister to widows?

A. Men can do things like helping with oil changes and car up keep; things around the widow's home that needs fixed, advising them on large purchases or important financial decisions.

Women can assist by helping to clean a widow's house, going through her husband's things, cooking a home-cooked meal, putting together gift bags for them and taking them to doctor's appointments or grocery shopping.

Youth can help with lawn work, washing her car, lifting heavy things, and baking for them.

Children can make cards for; Valentine's Day, Christmas, etc.

CHAPTER 8

ADDITIONAL RESOURCES

In the following pages you will find additional resources that you can use as you begin your widows' ministry, some of which were referenced in earlier chapters. **You can also find digital versions of these resources on our website at:**
http://widowslink.org/programresources.

Here is a list of the resources in this chapter:

- Widow Care Package Ideas
- First Things First
- Communicating with Recent Widows
- How to Communicate with a Grieving Widow
- The Widow's Promise Basket
- Widows' Advice of Dos and Don'ts
- Wings for Widows

WIDOW CARE PACKAGE IDEAS

* Used by permission from Widow Might (https://www.widowmight. org/care-package-ideas/).

- Provide a meal in a disposable container (be sure to note whom it is from but requesting that no thank-you note be written). It is a blessing to be released from this burden for a time.
- Invite her out for coffee or dinner, with a listening ear included.
- Give her gift cards to local restaurants.
- Buy her a book (see Book Suggestions list in chapter 7).
- Provide free babysitting, if applicable, so she can have a little time away for herself.
- Offer to help drive kids to their activities.
- Send a card or letter in the mail to encourage her and let her know that you are praying for her.
- Invite her to see a movie.
- Give her a journal and consider writing a short note on the first page.
- Provide for an inexpensive getaway for rest.
- Give her a massage gift card (physical touch is healing and helps with relaxation).
- Give her a manicure or pedicure gift card.
- Give her a small birthday or Christmas gift (she may have lost the only person who gave her gifts).

- Send a note on the anniversary of her husband's death and/or their wedding anniversary (these dates are often overlooked or forgotten).
- Pray for and reach out to her kids (ministering to them ministers to her).
- Make a point to invite, and keep inviting, her and her family for dinner and other outings.

FIRST THINGS FIRST

The following article will help guide a widow through the many transitions that can occur in the beginning of her journey.

* Used by permission from Widow Might (https://www.widowmight. org/first-things-first/).

Major Life Changes

- In general, it is recommended that you avoid making major life changes, such as selling your home, or changing jobs, for at least one year.
- If you're concerned about your job, ask your HR department about taking a leave of absence or reducing your hours for a period of time.
- It's natural to question whether you should stay in your home – memories and familiar things will trigger your emotions, and seem to intensify your pain. This is a normal thing to happen while you grieve. If possible, try to give it time. Consider having someone stay with you for a while, or perhaps, you could stay with a friend or family member for a time, to help ease you back into your home without your husband.

Legal Matters

- Contact your attorney right away. If you don't have an attorney, ask a trusted friend or family member for a recommendation.

- Your attorney will guide you through pertinent issues, including:
  - Titles to your home, automobile, and other property
  - Insurance policies
  - Bank accounts
  - Credit Cards
  - Dependent issues

Finances

- Contact your financial planner right away. If you don't have one, ask a trusted friend or family member for a recommendation.
- Your financial advisor will guide you through issues such as:
  - Gathering and reviewing all statements
  - Notifying all institutions
  - Modifying accounts and service providers
  - Tax considerations
- Identify recurring bills by referring to the last 6-12 months of bank statements.
- Order 5-10 death certificates. You may need original death certificates for financial/banking accounts, creditors, and life insurance policies.
- Cancel your husband's check cards and credit cards – although this is emotionally hard to do, it needs to be done to prevent fraud.
- Request a free credit report for both you and your husband.

Life Insurance

- Most financial notifications can wait, but a life insurance settlement is typically fairly easy to apply for.
- **Do not invest life insurance proceeds, or pay off any large debts immediately.**
  Take time to make these big decisions and seek the advice of your financial planner.
- Many companies offer life insurance to their employees. Contact your husband's HR department to find out if he had a policy through his employer.

Social Security

- Notify Social Security of your husband's death. Visit the Social Security website for more information. You and your dependent children may be eligible for benefits.

Health

- Grief may negatively impact your ability to sleep. Incorporate healthy habits for improving your sleep and overall health.
- If your health insurance was held through your husband's employer, contact his HR department as a first step.
- Your financial planner may be able to provide information regarding personal health insurance options for the future.

Emotions

- If you are having suicidal thoughts, get help immediately. Do not wait. Call 911 or the LoveLines Crisis Ministry Connection at 612-379-1199.
- Depression, severe emotions, and mood swings are very normal while you grieve. It is helpful to get professional help during this time.
- Be aware that some prescription drugs may cause thoughts of suicide, increased anxiety, and other side effects that can exacerbate symptoms of grief. Investigate the side effects of any prescription drugs before you start taking them.

Household

- Be sure you know how to shut off the electricity, water, and natural gas in case of an emergency.
- Gather numbers of repair and service providers before you need them. Ask friends and family members to help you do this.

COMMUNICATING WITH RECENT WIDOWS

By JoLeta Nash (Missionary Associate with Widows Link)

When initially alerted to a death:

- Send a short text or a very brief message via Facebook Messenger if you have this information. ("I'm so sorry to hear about _____. I'm praying you sense the Lord surrounding you with His comfort both now and in the coming days.")
- Send a card with a note of sympathy.
- Drop something by the house (i.e., bagels, fruit, casserole, dessert, or paper goods).
- Put a notation in your calendar on the death date (phone or paper). This is so you can contact the widow next year to say, "I'm thinking of you today . . ." Consider making a note on the one-month, three-month, and six-month dates as well.
- Attend the funeral if you are able.
- Try not to bring up the term *widow* or say anything about ministry to widows at this time. It's too soon, and most haven't even thought of themselves as a "widow" yet.

Weekly for the first month:

- Send a text or a message on social media. ("You're in my thoughts and prayers this morning, so I wanted to check in on you . . .")

- If texting or messaging is not an option, call them.
- If you are headed to the store, ask if there is anything you can pick up for them while you are out.
- Send an additional card or two during the first month to say, "I'm thinking of you/praying for you . . ."
- Again, this is too soon to make reference to "widow," so avoid doing so.

One month after death:

- Communicate via phone call, card, text, or FB Messenger.
- In addition to saying, "I'm thinking of you/praying for you," also say, "When you are up to it, I would love to take you to lunch or dinner."
- Make sure you follow up after their response so they do not feel like they have been forgotten or dropped.

Beyond one month:

- Check in with them at least monthly (can be weekly, or every two weeks—whatever works for the situation/relationship).
- When they are ready, offer to take them out for a meal. You may let them choose where to eat (if they want to), and help make them feel like the most important person that day. You can give them a book on widowhood or a helpful devotional, especially one on the Psalms. Share with them about any upcoming widow events and invite them to be your guest. Try not to be pushy; just

invite them. It varies greatly as to when they are ready to identify with a group of widows. Also let them know of any grief groups, like GriefShare, meeting in your area.

- Make a point to contact them on specific dates (birthday, anniversary, six months from spouse's death, and one year from spouse's death).

- It's nice to remember them on their birthday, anniversary, and spouse's death date each year as possible. If you can, learn to allow the widow to dictate how you progress down this list. Many are initially thankful that you are calling them, but they don't want much interaction. Continue to check on them periodically, and in time, most will become more open to meeting with you or to joining a group. Sending a card or reaching out with a phone call or text means more to most ladies than we realize—especially remembering the important dates is huge to widows, especially when most everyone seems to have forgotten. Widows will long remember those who have kept in touch with them and taken an interest in their new journey of widowhood. They will remember when someone takes the time to make their lives easier in some small (or big) way.

- Over time, it is very fulfilling to see the transformation in a widow's life as they are loved and given care. You are helping her to heal and to find hope and her new purpose in life.

HOW TO COMMUNICATE WITH A GRIEVING PERSON

You may be hesitant to approach a person grieving the death of a family member or friend. Not knowing what to say, you may tend to avoid this person at the time he or she needs your support. In doing so, you may unintentionally hurt the person deeply. There is not a formula or simple way to approach a grieving person. It is your heart of concern and love that you need to express. Be genuine. Be authentic, and say what you really mean. There is no way to say "just the right thing" to make it all okay. There are no magical words to take the hurt away. There is a difference between pity (you are a victim) and empathy (I understand, and I am with you).

HERE ARE SOME HELPFUL SUGGESTIONS

- Remain calm and nonjudgmental.
- Use direct and specific language (time, place, people surrounding) to help them reorient.
- Encourage people to talk about what happened prior to the death.
- Mention the deceased by name.
- Show your humanity; be honest about how you feel.
- Make several short visits.
- Don't take over the decision-making process. Let the grieving people make plans (but do be prepared to inter-vene if you genuinely believe a decision is inappropriate or ill-advised).
- Be willing to listen, especially in the evening.
- Let them cry and express their emotions.
- Visit during the weeks after the funeral when others get back to normal life but those grieving can't. (Be there for them when everyone else has moved away.)
- Minister to the whole family, but don't let them latch on in an unhealthy manner.
- If the bereaved want to talk about their loss, don't change the subject to a lighter topic.
- Don't say that you know how they feel. Each loss is unique.
- Don't be afraid to gently touch them in an appropriate manner. Hugs are often especially appreciated!
- Take your conversation cues from them. Silence is okay.
- Don't tell the bereaved how good they look to avoid talking about how bad they feel.

Tell your grieving friend about GriefShare, a grief recovery support group program that meets in churches around the world and online. At GriefShare, people find comfort, help, support, and direction as they navigate their journey of grief. To find a group, go to griefshare.org or call 800-395-5755.

THE WIDOW'S PROMISE BASKET

The Widow's Promise Basket is a gift of love and compassion given to a widow a month or two after her spouse dies, not during the first few weeks when she is still receiving phone calls and casseroles.

Put together a basket with various items for the widow. Tie a tag to each item with Scripture references of appropriate promises from God's Word. A list of gifts and corresponding verses are on the following pages. You may think of other promises to include. Permission is granted to copy this page to make tags—white or colored cardstock works well.

Created by Lynn Bowman who spent over twenty years honoring and caring for widows.

ITEMS FOR THE BASKET

1. A new crisp one dollar bill
2. Set of pillowcases
3. Small heart dish/item
4. A candle
5. A comb
6. Teacup with tea bags
7. Small package of tissue

1

"My God will meet all your needs according to His glorious riches in Christ Jesus."

Philippians 4:19

2

"When you lie down, you will not be afraid; when you lie down your sleep will be sweet."

Proverbs 3:24

3

"Because the Lord's great love we are not consumed, for His compassions never fail. They are new every morning: great is your faithfulness."

Lamentations 3:22-23

4

"The Lord is my light and my salvation—whom shall I fear? The Lord is the stronghold of my life- of whom shall I be afraid?"

Psalm 27:1

5

"And even the very hairs on your head are all numbered. So don't be afraid; you are worth more than many sparrows."

Matthew 10:30-31

6

"To know the love of Christ that surpasses knowledge-that you may be filled to the measure of all the fullness of God."

Ephesians 3:19

7

"He will wipe every tear from their eyes. There will be no more death or mourning or crying or pain."

Revelation 2:14

This little basket is filled with items representing the promises of God. As you use these items, please know I am praying for you. Most importantly, know that God loves you and His promises never fail.

GIFT BOOK SUGGESTIONS:

For women: *A Widow's Journey* by Gayle Roper

For men: *Experiencing Grief* by H. Norman Wright

OTHER THINGS YOU CAN INCLUDE:

Candy, Mints, Flashlight, Use your imagination.

This will be a special gift for the widow or widower and a way to remind them they are loved by you and by the Lord.

WIDOWS' ADVICE OF DOS AND DON'TS

* Used by permission from Widow Might (https://www.widowmight.org/dos-and-donts/).

DO . . .

- Do call and check in with me every few days, especially the first six months.
- Do offer to help and be as specific as possible. Tell me what you would like to help us with (errands, home maintenance, meal preparation, etc.) and what times work for you.
- Do offer to babysit or help carpool if I have kids at home.
- Do help me find qualified professionals to help make big decisions/actions.
- Do assist with problem solving such as car repair, home repair, choosing a lawn service, etc.
- Do research, provide qualified options and give me your opinion, but allow me to make the final decision.
- Do offer to accompany me to appointments and places that may be difficult for me to go to alone.
- Do watch my physical appearance and go shopping with me for a new outfit when my size changes.
- Do encourage me to get the help I need, which may include support groups or counseling.
- Do be forgiving, loving, and empathetic.
- Do give me extra grace, as the whole world has shifted under me.

- Do show me compassion and care, and realize that I am very vulnerable right now.
- Do stand with me and encourage me as I venture into the world again.
- Do help me to believe in myself. It's hard, but I can do this.
- Do keep loving and praying for me.
- Do follow through and do whatever you tell me you are going to do.

DON'T . . .

- Don't be afraid to tell me that you have no idea what to say.
- Don't say you know exactly what I am going through.
- Don't be afraid to give me a hug.
- Don't tell me I am strong; it shuts me down from sharing what is really going on and makes me feel like I have to do everything alone.
- Don't assume I will call when I need help with something. Be proactive and offer to help with specific tasks or offer a specific time when you can help out.
- Don't be afraid to mow my lawn or clear the snow from my driveway.
- Don't avoid talking about my husband. I love to hear stories about him.
- Don't take it personally if I forget birthdays, appointments, etc.
- Don't be afraid to include me in get-togethers where other couples will be present.

- Don't ask how I am unless you would like an honest answer.
- Don't expect me to help you deal with your grief as I can barely handle my own.
- Don't judge that I am grieving too much or too little.
- Don't be discouraged if your offer to help is met with a "no." Keep contacting and keep visiting.
- Don't wait for someone else to step up. If you can do it, do it! And do it now.
- Don't assume things are better just because months have gone by. Grieving is a long process.
- Don't take my depression and negativism personally. Continue to love me unconditionally and consistently. Be present and available.

Our Mission
We provide personalized financial wellness coaching to help the newly widowed move forward with confidence and hope.

You Are Not Alone.
We Can Help.
When life changes, we change lives

"I'm scared. And angry! I just lost the one person in the world I trusted. The love of my life – my entire support system – is gone. I've seen the lists of all the things that I'm supposed to do, but nobody tells you how to do it. Where do I start? I need advice I can trust. It's all just so overwhelming.

When you don't know what to do or where to start, *Wings for Widows* can help.

Think of *Wings for Widows* as the "emergency room" for the newly widowed, where we treat financial trauma. Every new widow experiences some level of financial trauma after losing a spouse. And there's the administrative side of loss – the overwhelming list of things to do. *Wings for Widows* helps you navigate through the most uncertain, frightening, and stressful time in your life when you need trusted advice the most. And we never charge for our services.

I am so glad I reached out. They helped me to wrap my arms around the enormity of my situation and move forward with confidence. I can't thank them enough. Such a great resource!
~ Jo N., Eden Prairie MN

69% OF WIDOWS AND WIDOWERS
SAID THAT BECOMING THE SOLE FINANCIAL DECISION-MAKER WAS THE TOP FINANCIAL CHALLENGE OF WIDOWHOOD.[1]

The American College State Farm Center, Survey on Widows and Widowers Topline Report, July 2016.

The Right People.
Help You Can Trust.
The standard of excellence

A financial coach is a professional who works to understand your current situation and provide education and guidance to help you work toward a state of financial wellness and security. Financial coaching is simply the process of your working with your financial coach to improve your financial situation.

If They're Not a CFP® Pro, You Just Don't Know.

Wings for Widows financial coaches are licensed financial professionals. In fact, all our coaches have earned their CERTIFIED FINANCIAL PLANNER™ credentials. Not only can they provide the financial advice you desperately need, but they also have extensive experience in financial planning.

Wings for Widows pairs you with a pro bono CFP® Pro. We service all 50 states, so there is a CFP® Pro waiting to help you wherever you are.

> ❝ *Wings for Widows is a wonderful organization for anyone going through a loss of a spouse. They are compassionate, caring, and know how to address any type of situation. My coach Melissa was great!* ❞
> ~ *Kari T., Prosper TX*

Benefits of Financial Coaching
Let's get you back on your financial feet

There are many benefits to one-on-one financial coaching:

- Understand your financial priorities
- Feel a sense of accomplishment
- Have less anxiety
- Feel in control of your situation
- Improve your creditworthiness

- Be prepared for financial emergencies
- Feel confident that your family is protected
- Avoid legal problems
- Avoid making bad decisions
- Have a clearer picture of the future

> ❝ *I can now say I'm done dealing with paperwork and have the confidence that my future is secure financially. I highly recommend Wings for Widows to every widow, regardless of financial circumstances, in a time of overwhelming grief.* ❞
> ~ *Cindy K., Lakeville, MN*

You will receive *The Widow's Guide to Financial Wellness* workbook FREE when you work with your CFP® Pro. All coaching is virtual, allowing you to invite a trusted friend or family member to join you. 100% safe and confidential.

WINGS FOR WIDOWS

290 Peavey Road · Wayzata MN 55391
612-466-2716 · 888-946-4749

For more information, visit us at:
www.wingsforwidows.org

 /wingsforwidows    /wingsforwidows    /wingsforwidows

 YouTube
www.youtube.com/channel/UCvtdiTgawc27MPYwRWOUrNA

ABOUT THE AUTHOR

Widows are individuals within our communities and even our churches who have been overlooked and disregarded since the very first century (Acts 6:1). Marlene Craft spent almost thirty years in full-time pastoral ministry with her husband before his sudden passing at age fifty-five. God then gave Marlene a new vision for ministry, and Widows Link was born. Within a month of her husband's passing, Marlene knew she wanted to minister to widows. She felt the Lord told her that first she had to heal well, because hurting people cannot help hurting people. The church she attended had just begun a GriefShare program. Marlene went through the sessions three times and then worked on their leadership team for two years.

After that she began a small group ministry to widows at her church. As Marlene saw the healing that took place in the lives of those widows, it became her passion to equip other churches to do the same. Three years after starting the small group, she took the steps to become the first U.S. Missionary to Widows for the Assemblies of God. This gave her the means to travel the country to assist churches in beginning a widows' ministry.

One month after she became a fully appointed missionary, the "bumps" began and slowed down her plans on the writing of the program. Thirty days after celebrating becoming a missionary, Marlene was diagnosed with leukemia. Thankfully, it was a slow-growing, less aggressive form of the disease, so doctors planned on just observing her. Seven months later she ended up with a rare case of giant cell arteritis, in which she became totally blind in her left eye. After a biopsy and just two days before the second Widows Link Widows Cruise, she found out that the blindness was permanent. This didn't slow down Marlene's heart to equip the church and minister to widows. A year later she had two separate heart ablations and ended up losing two-thirds of her spleen to leukemia a year after that. Despite the many "bumps" along the way, Marlene's heart has stayed firm to finish this book that you hold in your hands today.

It is all because of God's great heart for widows and His command for the church to care for them (James 1:27) that Marlene has not let anything stop her work on behalf of widows. Now you, too, can go and live out pure and genuine religion by caring for widows in your community.

ENDNOTES

1. "Marital Status of the United States Population in 2021, By Sex," Statista.com, accessed August 19, 2022, https://www.statista.com/statistics/242030/marital-status-of-the-us-population-by-sex/.

2. *Shall We Dance*, directed by Peter Chelsom, written by Masayuki Suô and Audrey Wells, featuring Richard Gere, Jennifer Lopez, and Susan Sarandon (New York: Miramax, 2004).

3. "Marital Status of the United States Population in 2021, By Sex," Statista.com, accessed August 19, 2022, https://www.statista.com/statistics/242030/marital-status-of-the-us-population-by-sex/.

4. Alicia Polk, "Top 10 Stressful Life Events," VitalsCounseling.com, July 29, 2018, https://vitaliscounseling.com/2018/07/19/top-10-stressful-life-events/.

5. "Marital Status of the United States Population in 2021, By Sex," Statista.com, accessed August 19, 2022, https://www.statista.com/statistics/242030/marital-status-of-the-us-population-by-sex/.

6. "Marital Status of the United States Population in 2021, By Sex."

7. "Marital Status of the United States Population in 2021, By Sex."